THE BLUEBIRDS

EVEN ON YOUR HAND!

Andrew M. Troyer

Acknowledgements
A special thanks to my dear family for their patience.
Also many thanks to James R. Hill, III and Richard Stevick for editing,
and to all others who, in any way or form, helped to produce this booklet.
My hand to you!

Additional copies available:
The Birds' Paradise
Rt. 3 Box 72, Conneautville, PA 16406

Table of Contents

1. The Beautiful Bluebirds 3
2. The Bluebirder's Ten Commandments 7
3. What is a Bluebird Trail 8
4. Why Have a Bluebird Trail 8
5. How and Where to Mount Your Bluebird Houses 9
6. Other Species That May Use Your Bluebird Houses 12
7. How and Why to Control the Bluebird's #1 Nest-site Competitor 18
8. Other Bluebird Enemies and How to Control Them 21
9. How to Monitor and Maintain Your Bluebird Trail 25
10. How and Why to Keep Field Records 26
11. Raising Your Own Mealworms 27
12. How to Train Wild Bluebirds to Feed From Your Hand ... 29

First printing January 1995
Second (revised) printing February 1996
Third Printing January 1999
Fourth Printing November 2004

Photos by John Nisley; B. Randall (VIREO); H.P. Smith, Jr. (VIREO); Robert Orthwein; James R. Hill, III; Mose J. Schwartz; and Orrson Farms.
Front and back cover photos: John Nisley.
Blueprint drawings: Dwight Haskell.

© Andrew M. Troyer 1994. All rights reserved.

No reproductions of any parts, in any form, may be used without written permission from the author.

ISBN 0-9642548-4-0

Printed in the United States of America

Carlisle Printing
OF WALNUT CREEK ltd.
2673 TR 421, Sugarcreek, OH 44681

The Beautiful Bluebirds

The Eastern Bluebird is a bird that shortens the long winters. Already on a sunny (may even be very cold) February day, as you walk the open country, you can hear their most beautiful song as they fly high overhead. They are already taking steps to establish their nesting territories. Winter boredom now has left, because their song has told me, in such a lovely way, that spring is just around the corner.

A young bluebird is being fed by its mother soon after fledging.

The Eastern Bluebird is not the "bluebird" (Blue Jay) that visits your regular feeding station. It is much smaller and does not usually mix in with regular feeder birds. It is slightly larger than the common House Sparrow, and is a cousin to the American Robin. The male can be seen on the front, and the female on the back, cover of this booklet. As you can see, the male is much deeper sky blue than the female. Bluebirds are kept busy raising two to three broods per season, from March until August. The female lays from three to six light blue eggs per clutch and incubates them from twelve to fourteen days. Approximately 5% of the

A Western Bluebird (male) bringing food to its nestlings.

clutches are of white eggs instead of blue. Both the male and female feed the young for about eighteen days, then they fledge (leave the nest). Both parents teach their fledglings how to hunt for insects. In addition, the female builds most of the next nest. Fledglings have been seen helping their parents feed the second and/or third broods.

There are two other species of bluebird in North America. They are the Western Bluebird and the Mountain Bluebird. See their pictures (on pages 4 and 5) and the regional range map (on page 6).

Bluebirds have a voracious appetite for insects and that alone is a welcome addition to your backyard. But in winter, they feed on many kinds of wild berries, such as multiflora rose, autumn olive, wild sumac, etc. If these food sources are available, bluebirds will not migrate south.

I dare say that without man's help, bluebirds couldn't survive in today's world. The reason is loss of nesting cavities. In today's environment, the wooden fence posts, in which bluebirds used to nest, have been replaced by metal ones. And there are far fewer small farms with apple orchards, supplying numerous other natural nesting cavities.

In addition to these changes, bluebirds also have to deal with the very aggressive European Starling and House Sparrow that were introduced into North America in the 1800s. These aliens steal almost every natural cavity that is left. Fortunately, starlings can be eliminated from a bluebird trail by controlling the size of the entrance hole or slot in bluebird houses. Unfortunately, the House Sparrow is smaller than a bluebird, so other steps must be taken. Today, the bottom line is, bluebirds need our help. Let's give them a willing hand. ✧

A Mountain Bluebird (male) bringing food to its nestlings in a natural cavity.

Approximate Regional Range Maps

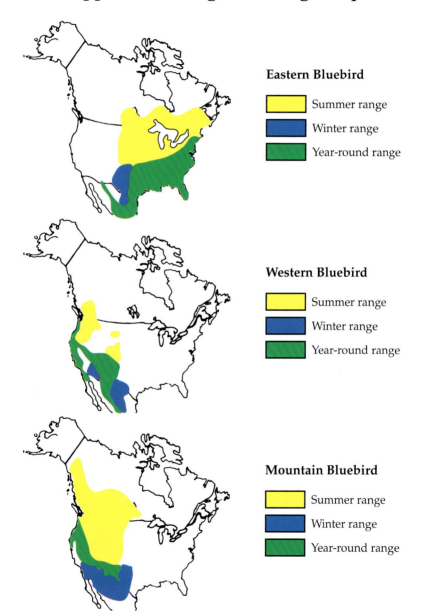

The Bluebirder's Ten Commandments

I. Place houses at least 300 feet apart, because bluebirds are territorial.

II. Keep the bluebird houses in open habitat. It's the environment they prefer.

III. Control the House Sparrow, or it will eliminate the bluebird and Tree Swallow.

IV. Add a second bluebird house 21 feet (7 paces) from the first house, at every 300-foot setting. This will allow the valuable Tree Swallow to also nest on your bluebird trail.

V. Control the most threatening parasite, the blowfly larva. If you don't, you may end up fledging very few, if any, baby birds.

VI. Attach a predator guard to your bluebird houses. This will protect the bluebirds from their predators and other enemies.

VII. Avoid handling the bluebird and/or Tree Swallow young after they are 14 days or older. They may fledge prematurely, which could cause their death.

VIII. Monitor your bluebird trail at least once every week.

IX. Remove the old bluebird and/or Tree Swallow nests on your first nest check after the young have fledged.

X. Keep accurate field records. This is the first step toward achieving greater success on your bluebird trail.

What is a Bluebird Trail

A bluebird trail is simply two or more bluebird houses placed in any rural area. The route you ride, drive, or walk to monitor and maintain them is called *your bluebird trail*. A typically-sized trail is made up of 10 to 50 houses, but the largest known trail is 2,000 miles long and contains thousands of houses. ✧

Why Have a Bluebird Trail

Bluebirds are not colonial-nesting birds like Purple Martins. Instead, they are territorial nesters. Each single pair of bluebirds will defend their nesting territory by not allowing other bluebirds to trespass within approximately a 150-foot radius of their nest. For this reason, if you want to attract more than one pair, you will need to establish a bluebird trail by placing your bluebird houses at least 300 feet apart.

Be very careful in choosing the size of your trail. The proper size should be no greater than the number of houses you can adequately monitor once a week.

Remember: The person who puts out just two houses, but cares properly for them, does *great!* The person who puts out fifty houses in the spring, but checks them only in the fall, does far more harm than good. *That person is raising pesty House Sparrows.*

By managing a bluebird trail, you are enriching your environment. Besides, it's a really great hobby! It can be competitive, such as certain groups, or clubs, competing to fledge the most young per season. Or it can be non-competitive, such as only one person giving the bluebirds a helping hand. It's a hobby for both males and females, young and old. No matter how you look at it, you can't lose. Managing a bluebird trail keeps the elderly exercised, the young out of mischief, and for us that are middle-aged, it releases stress. The bottom line is, it's the *only* way to bring back these precious *gems of blue.* ✧

How and Where to Mount Your Bluebird Houses

Great care should be taken in choosing the proper habitat when establishing your bluebird trail. Bluebirds prefer to feed in short, grassy areas such as pastures, lawns, cemeteries, recreational areas, etc. Please keep in mind *not* to place houses in any of the above mentioned areas if herbicides and/or pesticides, in any form, are used there. Bluebirds cannot tolerate such poisons.

Do not place houses directly in pastures. Cattle and horses will rub against them. This will break the birds' eggs and damage the bluebird houses. The solution to this is to place them $1^1/_2$ to 2 feet *outside* the pasture fence (see photo below). In this case the animals can't do harm and the

Pastures are the preferred habitat of bluebirds and Tree Swallows.

houses are close enough to the fence that they will not cause the farmer any problems working his fields on that side of the fence. Face the bluebird houses east to southeast. *Reasons:* The houses will get morning sunlight through their entrance holes, which helps warm the young after cool nights, and will also face the entrance holes away from most storms.

Before placing bluebird houses on other people's properties, be sure to get permission and inform them of what you are planning to do. Tell them that having bluebirds will help them get rid of unwanted insects and will add aesthetic value to their properties. *Remember:* Your neighbors will show you only as much respect as you show them. Always be very courteous.

Bluebird houses should be mounted only on metal posts. For the best and most economical mounting post, salvage used $3/4$" or 1" by $6^1/2$' long pipe. **Never mount your houses directly on fence posts, tree trunks or telephone poles.** This only lets predators climb up to them.

Drill a $1/4$" hole through the mounting post, at least 1" down from the top, so when the post is driven into the ground the hole stays round. Use a post driver or a sledge hammer and drive the post approximately $1^1/2$' into the ground until the mounting hole is at *your* eye level (see photo #1 and #5 on page 11). This mounts the bluebird house at the proper height for you to observe the nest when monitoring. The one-bolt mounting idea is the most economical mount I have ever seen. I know you will agree.

Drill two $1/8$" holes through the end-cap, then screw it to the bottom of the house's back (see photo #2 on page 11).

For an effective predator guard, put an 18" x 6" piece of PVC pipe down over the mounting post. In the center of the PVC end-cap, drill a hole just large enough for the mounting post to be inserted (see photo #3 on page 11). Paint the predator guard a color that blends in with the environment. It makes the entire structure less conspicuous to vandals, and protects the guard from ultraviolet rays. Next, drill a $1/4$" hole through the exact center of the house's back. Put a $1/4$" x 3" carriage bolt through the inside of the house, with the threads sticking out the back. Now lift the house with the end-cap screwed to the bottom and insert the mounting post through the center hole in the end-cap (see photo #3 on page 11). Then insert the 3" bolt through the hole in the mounting post and tighten it with a flat washer and wing nut. Lift the PVC predator guard up and slip it into the end-cap (see photo #4 on page 11). Do not glue. Use only one screw through the wall of the end-cap to attach it to the PVC guard. Use caulking to seal the hole around the mounting post on the top of the end-cap (again see photo #4 on page 11). Caulking will make the guard ant-proof. The end-cap actually stabilizes the lower part of the house. ✧

> *Always give your bluebirds the predator protection with a guard*

The one-bolt mounting idea works great for *ANY TYPE* of bluebird housing.

The exact height of a bluebird house is not critical, so mount your houses at eye level for *your* monitoring convenience.

Other Species That May Use Your Bluebird Houses

Besides the bluebird, the most valuable species that will use your house is the Tree Swallow. It is very competitive with the bluebird in claiming nesting cavities. If only single bluebird houses are placed every 300 feet, a Tree Swallow may come along and fight off and de-

An adult Tree Swallow. Notice the many small captured insects in its beak. Their legs make it look like the Tree Swallow has whiskers!

Young, nestling Tree Swallows almost ready for fledging.

stroy the bluebird's nest, then build its own. Or a bluebird may come along and fight off the Tree Swallow and destroy their nest, and build its own. Tree Swallows are also territorial, but only defend a nesting territory with about a 25' radius, whereas the bluebird defends a territory with about a 150' radius. The solution to their competition is quite simple. Just add a second house at every 300' setting by placing it approximately 21 feet (7 paces) from the first. With this spacing strategy, Tree Swallows will not drive away bluebirds, and bluebirds will not drive away Tree Swallows, on your bluebird trail. It is important to turn paired houses slightly toward each other so both competing occupants can see each other by looking out their entrance holes or slots. Doing so will minimize their aggression towards each other. The bluebird will take only one of the two houses, and then, if a Tree Swallow comes along, or vice versa, the fight doesn't last long. The newcomer just takes the second house.

While bluebirds and Tree Swallows do compete for nest cavities, they do not compete for food. Bluebirds capture spiders and insects from the ground, while Tree Swallows capture only flying insects caught in the air. For this reason, the two species can successfully nest close together.

Another species, the House Wren, may also use your bluebird houses. If you do not wish to nest this species, be sure to place your houses approximately 200 feet from all wooded and/or brushy areas. Wrens get nervous in open territories, and therefore will not choose to nest in such areas.

The nests of the above mentioned birds are distinguished as follows:

The bluebird's nest is a low, cup-shaped structure made of fine grasses or pine needles, with no feathers. They have blue eggs, although 5% of their clutches are of white eggs.

The Tree Swallows's nest is also a low, cup shaped structure, but it has lots of precisely placed feathers. Their eggs are always pure white in color.

The House Wren's nest is always bulky and made of twigs. Their eggs are reddish spotted.

Titmice and chickadees may also use your bluebird houses, but this is far less common because they prefer wooded areas.

The least desired species to have in your bluebird house is the House Sparrow. Their very bulky nests are made of grasses and feathers. It's quite common for them to have some grasses sticking out the entrance hole. Their eggs are grayish spotted.

A bluebird's nest with eggs.

A Tree Swallow's nest with eggs.

Bluebird Feeder Blueprints

Bluebirds are very inquisitive. Seemingly they will investigate any newly placed bluebird house in their acquainted area. While investigating such a feeder they will find the food. For this reason the bluebird house type feeder works best, especially to get the wild bluebirds trained to back or front yard feeding. Use the inside compartment for food storage, etc.

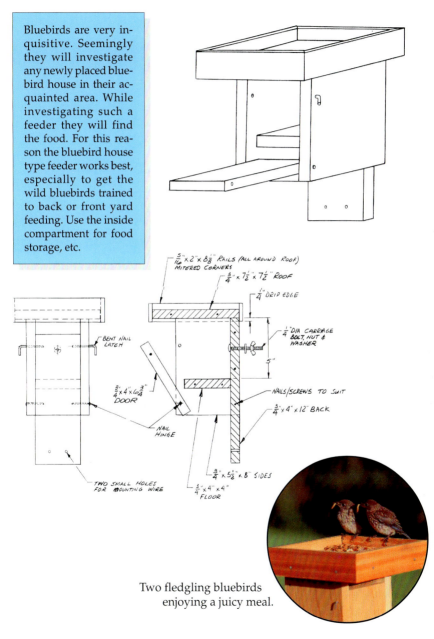

Two fledgling bluebirds enjoying a juicy meal.

In sparrow-free areas, use regularly-designed bluebird houses.

Troyers' Sparrow-Resistant Bluebird House

In sparrow-infested areas, use this shallow slot bluebird house with pull-out tray.

All parts are made from 3/4" thick wood except the gusset, back, and pull-out tray.

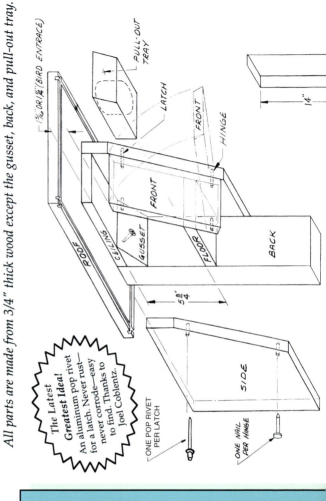

The Latest Greatest Idea! An aluminum pop rivet for a latch. Never rust—never corrode—easy to find. Thanks to Joel Coblentz.

What Makes this House Sparrow-Resistant?

Sparrows love to build a bulky nest over top of their nest and entrance. This compact house does not give them room enough to do so.

Why the Slot?

Bluebirds and Tree Swallows can escape when attacked by sparrows. The intruder cannot block the slot like a hole, which lets the birds exit to safety. Thus it saves many adult birds' lives. The intruder then sees there is not room enough for him to nest, so he usually lets the

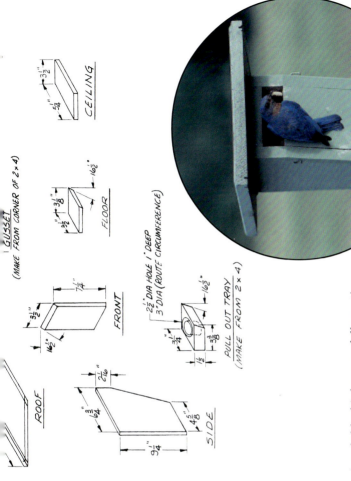

A male bluebird successfully nesting in a sparrow-infested area, in one of these sparrow-resistant bluebird houses.

Why the Gusset?

This is only to take up some extra cubic inches of inside space that sparrows would love, but bluebirds and tree swallows do not need.

Why the Pull-Out Tray with Sawdust?

The tray makes cleaning out easy. Bluebirds prefer deeper houses; so do sparrows, but the bluebirds do accept this shallow slot better than the sparrows. Tests indicate strongly that if bluebirds and Tree Swallows are bribed with a nice tray of sawdust, they will accept this shallow slot much more readily. It is only natural for a bird to be able to form its cup for the nest before bringing in nesting materials. What is at the bottom of every natural cavity? Yes, it is sawdust.

Bring Back the Bluebirds ✦ 17

How and Why to Control the Bluebird's #1 Nest-site Competitor

The bluebird's #1 nest-site competitor is the House Sparrow. This aggressive species was introduced to North America in the 1850s. These aliens are legally trapped in the United States and Canada. They are as undesirable as a mouse in your house. When trapped, *do not* take them miles down the road to be released. This is no different than throwing your garbage over the fence onto your neighbor's property. A very humane way to eliminate them is to put them into a plastic bag, then hold it to a car exhaust. The carbon monoxide kills them quickly and painlessly.

If you wish to have bluebirds and/or Tree Swallows, House Sparrows *must be controlled!!* Not only do they kill adult bluebirds and Tree Swallows, but they also break and kick out these birds' eggs. Sometimes, instead of kicking them out, they just build their nests right over top of them. The male House Sparrow does all the damage.

House sparrows must be controlled, or they will eliminate the bluebirds and Tree Swallows.

The alternative to controlling this nest-site competitor is to use the sparrow-resistant bluebird house (see blueprints on pages 16 and 17). We have found this house to be very effective. We recommend it for sparrow-infested areas only. In sparrow-free areas, use regularly-designed housing, since bluebirds have a slight preference for deeper compartments. The shallow depth is what plays the biggest role in making the house sparrow resistant. The slot is great for letting the bluebird or Tree Swallow escape, should a male House Sparrow investigate. This prevents many adult bluebirds and Tree Swallows from being killed by sparrows. What a treat it is to have a bluebird trail that is almost entirely sparrow free! ✧

Male House Sparrows kill adult bluebirds and Tree Swallows and their babies. They also break and throw out the eggs of both species.

An adult Eastern Bluebird killed by a male House Sparrow.

The alternative is using this sparrow-resistant bluebird house.
The blueprints are on pages 16 and 17.

John Nisley photo

In-House Sparrow Trap
Huber–Tuttle Design

This sparrow trap will fit inside any regularly designed bluebird house that has a front or side opening, even inside the Petersons style. It is to be used only after a sparrow has taken over your bluebird house.

It finger fastens onto the inside of the house's front. No screwdriver is needed. Sparrows can be trapped almost immediately if half of their nest is left below the trap, inside the bluebird house.

The reason for the $1^3/8$" hole is that in most cases the bluebirds cannot enter—only sparrows can.

The trap *must be checked daily!* It is sickening to find a trapped bluebird or Tree Swallow dead through negligence.

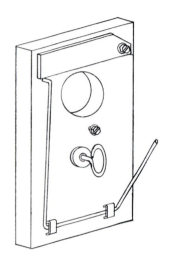

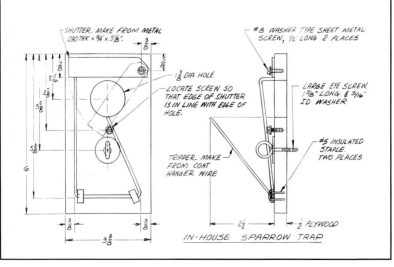

IN-HOUSE SPARROW TRAP

Other Bluebird Enemies and How to Control Them

What many people don't know is that blowfly larvae kill quite a number of young bluebirds and Tree Swallows if they aren't controlled. The adult female blowfly lays her eggs in the nests of bluebirds and Tree Swallows. These eggs hatch and become larvae. The larvae thrive only on the blood of young birds. They hide in the nesting material during the day, then come up and suck the blood from the young nestlings at night. Chemicals can be applied to kill these larvae, but if it's strong enough to kill insects, it's not safe to use around young birds. The solution to this is to change both species' nests when the young are seven to ten days old. At that time, remove the nest with young. Scrape out all dirt, larvae, etc. from the floor of the bird house. Take a generous

An adult blowfly.

Blowfly larvae.

Approximately eight-day-old bluebird babies ready for a nest change.

Using both thumbs works great to form the cup in a handmade nest.

handful of soft *dried* grass and make a new handmade nest. Four- to six-inch pieces of grass work best. Put both of your thumbs where you want the cup formed. Work the handful of grass around and around in your hands. While doing so, use both thumbs to form the cup of the nest (see photo above). Soon you will have a surprisingly well formed nest. Put this handmade nest inside the bluebird house, then gently place the young back into it.

By removing the old nest, you will have removed all the larvae, plus all the blowfly eggs that are actually invisible to the naked eye. Should a female blowfly come along and lay more eggs in your new handmade nest, it doesn't matter. By the time those eggs hatch and the larvae are able to do harm, the nestling birds will have fledged. You can even sleep better knowing those young now have comfort. I have never had, nor heard of, one parent ever abandoning one of these handmade nests. It's a 100% successful method of controlling nest parasites without the use of poisonous pesticides. In this way you can have chemically free nests with healthy young babies.

> *I have never had, nor heard of, one parent ever abandoning one of these handmade nests.*

Two other bluebird killers are herbicides and insecticides. If these are used by farmers in areas where bluebirds feed, you can expect to find lots of dead nestlings. Chemical weed-kill and lawn care products used by homeowners are just as bad, if not worse. *Birds are the barometer of the environment.* Healthy birds, healthy environment. Dead birds, I'll let you guess the rest.

To control predators such as raccoons, cats, snakes, mice, and even ants, use the predator guard described on pages 10 and 11.

One other potential problem is vandalism. Use your own judgment as to where to place your housing to prevent it. Sometimes, it may be your neighborhood children. If so, try to help them understand what they are doing to these beautiful creatures.

Also, explain how important it is to value and respect these native birds. Most of the time this is all it takes, but if not, you may have to move your houses. Always keep in mind that above every cloud there is sunshine! ✧

Bluebirds are very susceptible to poison chemicals because they are attracted to any poisoned squirming insect seen on the ground. Such insects are easily found foods for the bluebird babies. Thus, if poison chemicals are used in the nesting area, they're carried by the parents through the food chain to their young. This generally kills them. The Tree Swallows are just the opposite. They are hardly ever affected by the use of such herbicides and insecticides, because they eat only flying insects.

Dead bluebird young removed from nest after poisonous chemicals were used in the area.

How to Monitor and Maintain Your Bluebird Trail

You should monitor your bluebird trail once a week; yes, every seven days. Sometimes, you may even need to monitor certain houses in between.

If you have bluebird houses placed on other people's recreational areas, be sure to monitor your trail on a weekday. This is so you don't walk in on your neighbors while they are enjoying their weekend off. I've also found that landowners eagerly listen to my success from their land. These suggestions build up good relationships with your neighbors. This helps to establish a happy neighborhood with a healthy environment.

Try to have all your bluebird houses out soon after the winter's snow is gone. But houses put out as late as midsummer may still get bluebirds (bluebirds only). They nest two to three times during one season, whereas Tree Swallows nest only once per season, in the spring. You should leave some, if not all, of your bluebird houses out during the winter. The bluebirds need them for winter roosting. This gives them good protection in bad weather.

Clean and repair your bluebird houses annually. I do mine every spring just before the nesting season begins. The better you monitor and maintain your trail, the greater your success will be. ✧

Below is a list of items needed to monitor your bluebird trail effectively.

A BAG, with a carrying strap
SCREWDRIVER, for multiple uses
PUTTY KNIFE, for cleaning out old nests
WHITE PLASTIC LID FROM A TWO-GALLON ICE CREAM CONTAINER, to set in old nests, etc., for inspections
SMALL HAMMER, for multiple uses
A BAG OF DRIED GRASS, for your materials to make a new nest
A BAG OF SAWDUST, to put in tray after each clean-out
SOME NAILS, for multiple uses
SOME SCREWS, for multiple uses
A FEW NEW PLASTIC BAGS, to bring home specimens from nest inspections, etc.
A FIELD LIST, for keeping good records
A PENCIL, because pens do not always write outdoors

How and Why to Keep Field Records

Have you ever heard of a business succeeding without keeping good records? I haven't. It's the same in managing a bluebird trail. Only by keeping good field records can you know exactly what your changes or improvements amounted to. It's a great satisfaction to me, knowing how I'm doing in business, as well as on the bluebird trail.

Here is a simple, yet efficient, method of keeping field records (see below). At the end of the breeding season, you will find it helpful to total and summarize all your breeding data.

Field Records

# of Houses	4-18	4-25	5-2	5-9	5-16	5-23	5-30	6-6	6-13	6-20	6-27	7-4	7-11	7-18	7-25	8-1	8-8	8-15	8-22	8-29
Paired 1	BN	BE5	BE?	BY5	BY5 C	BY5	BY5 ④		BN	BE4	BE4	BY4	BY4 C	BY4	BY4 ④					
Paired 2		TN 1/2	TN	TE2	TE5	TE5	TY5	TY5 C	TY5	TY5 ④										
Paired 3		BN	BE5	BE5	BE2 BY3	BY4 C	BY4	BY4 ④		BN	BE4	BE4	BY4 C	BY4	BY2	BY2 ④				
Paired 4			TN	TEI	TE6	TE7	TY4 TE3	TY6 C	TY6	TY6 ④										

Annual Summary of my first four years at our new location in Conneautville, Pennsylvania.

	1991	1992	1993	1994	1995
# of houses offered	24 regular	30 regular	30 slots	30 slots	30 slots & 1 regular
# of BB eggs laid	60	71	51	84	66
# of BB eggs hatched	48	56	41	76	48
# of BB young fledged	30	41	36	48	44
# of TS eggs laid	58	67	65	82	92
# of TS eggs hatched	50	58	59	66	81
# of TS young fledged	42	35	59	53	62
% of BB eggs laid that fledged	50%	58%	71%	57%	67%
% of TS eggs laid that fledged	72%	52%	91%	65%	67%
# of paired houses occupied	14	18	2	14	8
# of sparrows trapped	23	35	0	0	0
# of nestlings lost to sparrows	13	10	0	0	0
# of nestlings lost to other	13	28	5	41	23
Total # of TS & BB fledged	72	76	95	101	106

Legend
Add more of your own codes if needed.

B = Bluebird
T = Tree Swallow
S = Sparrow
W = Wren
N = Nest
E = Eggs
Y = Young
④ = #Fledged
C = Nest Change
? = Female on Eggs

The bottom line (total) is doing very well here at our new location in Pennsylvania.

Raising Your Own Mealworms

Mealworms are the larvae of ground beetles. Bluebirds have a very strong appetite for these insects. Offering your bluebirds mealworms is like offering your children candies they can't resist. Follow these step-by-step instructions and enjoy raising your own bluebird food.

1. Find a clear plastic container with approximately six-inch high sides. It may be the size of one to three square feet. For ventilation, drill about forty $1/4$-inch holes in the lid. If condensation occurs, drill even more holes, or cover the container with a screen.

2. Put about three inches of one part chick starter (or laying mash) and one part wheat bran in the container. Both can be purchased at your local feed mill. Mix well and level it. This is food for your newly hatched mealworms.

3. Cut an apple in half. Turn the round side down and push it down into the feed until flush with the feed and bran mixture. This is to give them moisture. If the skin of the apple is removed, the moisture in it will get into your feed and will spoil it. For this reason, *do not* peel your apples. Check your cultures every week to make sure they aren't out of apples.

4. Add thirty to forty mealworms per square foot of container. Get them from your friends, or you can find them in a farmer's feed building, usu-

A newly started mealworm culture. Notice the half vitamin bottle with $1/4$" holes. This works great to sift the worms from culture contents.

ally under his feed bags. They can also be bought from Grubco, Inc. in Hamilton, Ohio (phone 1-513-874-5881). Add four layers of unprinted paper such as the regular brown grocery bags. Put paper on top of the feed mixture, apple halves, and mealworms. Mealworms love to hide between the layers of paper. I record the date I start each culture on the top layer of paper (see photo on page 27).

5. Store such a started culture at room temperature, or warmer. These mealworms will each turn into a pupa, then the pupa will turn into a beetle. These beetles will mate, then lay their eggs between the paper and feed. After this, the beetles die. This is their complete life cycle. Soon you'll see many tiny mealworms when you run your fingers through the top of the feed. They will produce up to 3,000 worms per square foot of container. This complete cycle will take only two to three months, if your culture is stored at, or slightly above, room temperature. Temperature plays a big role in the length of the beetle's life cycle. I start a new culture every month. This strategy keeps me in plenty of worms.

6. Replace the apples whenever they are completely eaten or half spoiled. After the young mealworms are seen, keep two halves, rather than only one half apple, per square foot of container. Keeping plenty of moisture (apples) available keeps the worms growing faster. Potatoes also work, but apples work better because they supply more moisture for the worms.

7. Put fully grown worms into another well-vented container with only some feed and a bit of apple. Store these in a cool place, or even in the refrigerator. This delays them from turning into a pupa for up to six months. Set container out to room temperature for one day every week to allow the worms to feed.

All baby birds will eat mealworms. They are very handy should you ever have to hand-feed an unfledged baby bird. They are also handy should you decide to go fishing. Bottom line—mealworms are just as exciting for birders to raise as flowers are for folks with a green thumb. Good luck!!! ✧

Mealworms are as appealing to bluebirds as candies are to children.

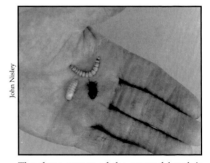

The three stages of the ground beetle's complete life cycle: mealworm, pupa, and then a beetle.

How to Train Wild Bluebirds to Feed From Your Hand

I will share with you my personal experiences of attracting bluebirds to my mealworm feeder, then onto my hand. I tried for more than five years to attract bluebirds to a feeder stocked with raisins and sunflower meats, but failed until I offered mealworms. Once I used these, it took less than thirty minutes. You, too, can succeed if you follow these ten steps.

1. Notice where your bluebirds like to perch whenever they are on your property.

2. Mount your bluebird feeder on a tripod or on a sharp-pointed, four-foot wooden or metal rod. This will allow your feeder to be portable so you can keep moving it closer to your preferred location. Place the feeder in the area mentioned in #1 and stock it with mealworms.

Immature bluebirds enjoying a snack of mealworms.

3. Keep offering mealworms until the bluebirds have found them. Soon they will know that the feeder is a place they can predictably find food.

4. Offer approximately ten worms per bird, twice a day. Find a specific time in the morning, and again in the evening, that fits your schedule. The bluebirds will soon adjust to your feeding routine. Be sure to whistle or ring a bell each time you put mealworms in the feeder. *Important:* Whichever sound you make, always do the same one. Your bluebirds will soon know that this means, "Dinner is ready!"

5. At this point, before feeding mealworms, give your dinner call, even at off feeding hours. Do this until you are sure they know what you are doing.

6. Now move your feeder toward your own dwelling. Twenty to thirty feet per day works fine. Do this until you have the feeder by a window that opens easily.

7. Get the bluebirds accustomed to this spot. Next, wait until bad weather (a low pressure) is present. The reason for this is because birds feed more aggressively during such times, and are less inhibited. Have an assistant put his or her hand out through the window, one foot above the feeder. Be sure to have the window, or its screen, pulled down against the assistant's arm. What you want is for the bluebirds to see only the assistant's hand outside, not the whole person inside. Now call the birds as usual, but put the mealworms on the assistant's hand instead of on the feeder. Then, back away just as usual. They should soon

A male bluebird enjoying his meal on a cold winter's day.

light upon the assistant's hand and eat.

8. After they have become accustomed to the handouts at the window, you will then be able to call them from the window and feed them without anyone outside.

9. Now try to hand-feed the bluebirds outside, next to the window. You may have to sit behind a shrub or lawn chair to get them to accept your hand on the outside. Before you know it, they will feed from your hands anywhere on your property. If I walk to the barn and whistle, they come, and then when I walk back to the house and whistle, they come again. They follow me around just like sheep follow their shepherd.

> *They follow me around just like sheep follow their shepherd.*

10. Keep your feeder by the window or in your front yard. At times, you may just want to put the mealworms in the feeder instead of hand feeding the birds. You may also add dogwood berries, autumn olive berries, or elderberries to their diet. Some of these must be harvested and frozen in the fall, then thawed before feeding in the winter. Offering berries helps conserve your mealworm supply.

As I have mentioned, bluebirds are territorial. This especially shows up when you are feeding them in the winter and the weather breaks in advance of spring. A dominant pair will drive all the others away and nest in the bluebird house closest to your feeding area. In the fall when nesting season is over and territorial defenses break down, more bluebirds will come in.

Last spring, whenever I'd whistle, the female bluebird that was incubating her eggs popped out of her house to get her meal. This was quite exciting, especially since she'd eat the mealworms right off our hands.

Last winter we had extremely severe weather conditions. Our bluebirds disappeared on January 7. We feared they had died. But on February 15, I noticed a pair perched on the wires. I thought these might be the same birds, so I quickly got some mealworms and whistled as I got to the driveway. Believe me, the male flew toward me. He knew me, and I knew him. The word spread very fast, because by evening we had a total of eight beautiful bluebirds. I was so thrilled that I gave them all the mealworms they could possibly eat.

When bluebirds are feeding their young, they love to take mealworms to them. If the young are still small, the parents break up the worms before feeding them to their nestlings. After the nestling bluebirds have fledged, the parents will make trip after trip with worms to the local trees where their fledglings are hiding. After they can fly better, the parents will bring them to the feeding area. They will take worms to them, get them all excited, then purposely drop the worms to teach them that food is found on the ground. Bluebirds train their fledglings, as we parents train our children. Interesting! After the young have learned that they can find food themselves, they will also eat at the feeder and, at times, right off your hands. I'm sure that you, too, will find that having a bluebird light upon your hand not only excites you, it inspires your soul.

When my friend, Richard Stevick, a Christian college professor from Messiah College, was visiting and hand-fed our bluebirds, he was so moved by the experience that he stated, "I felt like I was Adam, back in the Garden of Eden!" Professor Tim Moriarty described it as, "It was like a touch of Heaven."

Important!!! Do not stop feeding your bluebirds in the winter. Once you've trained them to feeding, they depend upon you for their food source. Should you run out of meal worms, call Grubco in Hamilton, Ohio at 1-513-874-5881. They ship their mealworms via UPS. Should you choose not to feed your bluebirds through the winter, just stop feeding them in late fall.

During long periods of bad weather, mealworms can also be placed on a feeder ten feet away from any nesting bluebird pair on your bluebird trail. This will supply them with food for their young and help reduce weather-related mortality.

Do you know the color of a first-prize ribbon? That's the same color that is on the backs of these precious gems. Let's give them a prize-winning helping hand and bring them back, perhaps even on *your* hand. ✧

> "I felt like I was Adam, back in the Garden of Eden!"
> —Richard Stevick
> Professor, Messiah College

Together, a male and female Eastern Bluebird are enjoying a handout.